July 2020. This book was created during the pandemic and sheltering in place. Being able to be in my backyard was my savior (everything in this book is from my backyard). Even though I have been working remotely, the families that I serve are in my thoughts. This book is for them.

ONE WHITE CHAIR

2

Two Red Chairs

Three Chairs...

1 White and 2 red equals 3 chairs

4

FOUR BICYCLES

FIVE POTTED PLANTS

Can you count how many pink petals?

SEVEN ROCKS

Eight Buddha faces. Can you count all by yourself?

9

Nine Pluots. If you eat one how many do you have left?

How many bunnies do you see? Your turn to count.

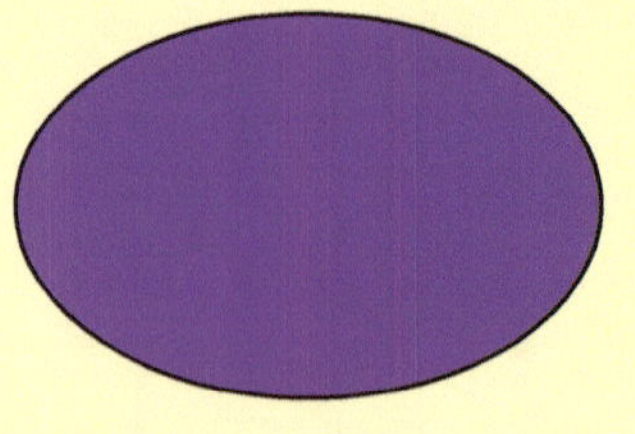

Shapes

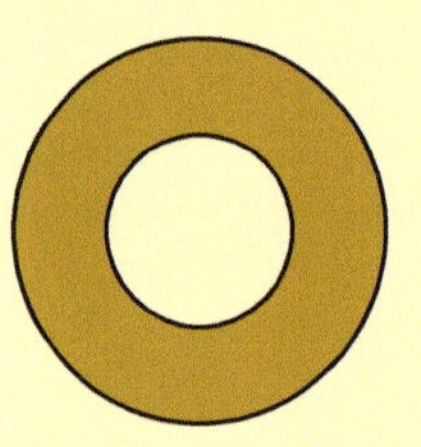

Heart

Trace the heart with your finger

Diamond

Star

Pentagon

How many sides do you see?

Circle

Square

Rectangle

Size Words

And

Math concepts

Long hose

Short Stick

Bunches of Grapes

Big chair

Little Chair

Round rock on top

Top heart is larger than bottom heart

Backyard Creatures

Dragonfly.....Can you count the wings?

Praying mantis...What shape is the head?

Snake

Do you see a heart on the frog?

How many flies do you see?

How many hummingbirds do you see?